KOALAS

by Sandra Lee

The Child's World

Content Adviser:
The Zoological Society
of San Diego

Published in the United States of America by The Child's World®
PO Box 326 • Chanhassen, MN 55317-0326
800-599-READ • www.childsworld.com

PHOTO CREDITS

© Daniel J Cox/naturalexposures.com: 9, 10, 11
© DiMaggio/Kalish/Corbis: 20
© D. Parer & E. Parer-Cook/Auscape/Minden Pictures: 19
© Eric and David Hosking/Corbis: 25
© Gary Bell/zefa/Corbis: 22–23
© John Shaw/Photo Researchers, Inc.: cover, 1
© Mark J. Thomas/Dembinsky Photo Associates: 4–5, 13
© Martin Harvey/Gallo Images/Corbis: 6–7, 14
© O. Alamany & E. Vicens/Corbis: 16–17
© Steve Kaufman/Corbis: 28
© Stuart Westmorland/Corbis: 27

ACKNOWLEDGMENTS

The Child's World®: Mary Berendes, Publishing Director;
Katherine Stevenson, Editor

The Design Lab: Kathleen Petelinsek, Design and Page Production

LIBRARY OF CONGRESS CATALOGING-IN-PUBLICATION DATA

Lee, Sandra, 1940–
  Koalas / by Sandra Lee.
    p. cm. — (New naturebooks)
  Includes bibliographical references and index.
  ISBN 1-59296-641-1 (library bound : alk. paper)
  1. Koala—Juvenile literature. I. Title. II. Series.
  QL737.M384L456 2006
  599.2'5—dc22   2006001369

3-4-08

Table of Contents

On the cover: This adult koala is climbing a eucalyptus tree in eastern Australia.

Meet the Koala!

Koalas have been around for about 15 million years. Koalas of long ago were much larger than the koalas of today.

A warm breeze blows through a forest in Australia. Leaves rustle as the branches sway back and forth. Between one of the branches and the tree's trunk, you can see a furry creature. Even though the tree moves gently in the breeze, the creature stays still—it's asleep! What is this sleepy animal? It's a koala!

Here you can see an adult koala as it sleeps on a sunny afternoon.

What Are Koalas?

The koala's closest animal relative is the wombat. Wombats are furry, burrowing animals with powerful legs for digging. Like koalas, wombats live only in Australia.

Many people think koalas are bears, but they are not. Instead, they belong to a group of animals called **marsupials**. Kangaroos and opossums are marsupials, too. Marsupials are animals that have a pocket of skin for carrying their babies. This pocket is called a **pouch**. Only female marsupials have pouches. A female koala's pouch is on her stomach.

Marsupials are also **mammals**. Mammals are animals that have warm blood, have fur or hair on their bodies, and feed their babies mother's milk. People, dogs, and cows are mammals, too.

These two koalas are watching the photographer from the safety of their tree.

What Do Koalas Look Like?

Koalas have extra-thick fur on their bottoms. The fur acts as a cushion and keeps the koalas comfortable when they sit for a long time.

Koalas in cooler areas are slightly larger and have thicker fur than koalas that live in warmer areas.

Koalas are covered with thick, gray fur. The fur is thick enough to be almost waterproof. Koalas have big ears that are covered with hair. They also have a rounded, leathery nose. Koalas also have a tail—but it is almost too short to see. Most adult koalas are a little over two feet (61 cm) tall and weigh about 20 pounds (9 kg).

This koala looks like a ball of fur as it sits on a branch. Koalas have the thickest fur of all marsupials.

Where Do Koalas Live?

Koalas tend to have several trees in which they spend most of their time. These "home trees" usually aren't visited by other koalas.

Male koalas have a special area on their chest that leaves a scent. They rub their chests on their "home trees" to leave their scent and mark the trees as their own.

Koalas live only in the eastern half of Australia. They live in forests of eucalyptus (yoo-kuh-LIP-tuss) trees. A koala's body is perfect for life in the trees. Each of its hands has two thumbs. These thumbs are ideal for grabbing branches. Sharp claws on the koala's hands and feet also help the animal climb.

Koalas move about by climbing across branches. When they want to move to a nearby tree, they leap across and use their claws to grab onto a branch. If the trees are farther apart, the koala must climb down the tree and walk on the ground to reach the new tree.

10

Koalas walk on all fours when they are on the ground. Opposite page: This young koala is munching on eucalyptus leaves.

What Do Koalas Eat?

Koalas eat a little over one pound (.5 kg) of leaves every day.

Like other plant-eating animals, koalas have mostly flat teeth for chewing.

Koalas are very fussy eaters. In fact, just about the only thing they will eat is eucalyptus leaves! Koalas will also eat acacia (uh-KAY-shuh) and melaleuca (mel-uh-LYOO-kuh) leaves, but eucalyptus leaves are by far their favorite.

There are many kinds of eucalyptus trees, but koalas eat the leaves of only a few types. They are even fussy about which leaves they eat. Before they eat a leaf, they carefully check and smell it. If it isn't quite right, they leave the leaf alone and move on to the next one.

This adult spent a long time sniffing these leaves before it finally decided to eat one!

Koalas aren't very active. They spend most of the day sleeping in the trees. When a sleepy koala moves, it often looks as if it's in slow motion. Why don't koalas have a lot of energy? It's because of their food. Eucalyptus leaves don't provide much energy, so koalas move slowly most of the time.

Koalas spend about 20 hours a day sleeping.

Male koalas are slightly more active than females. Males are also a little bigger.

If it needs to, a koala can move quickly. In zoos, it is sometimes difficult for keepers to catch a koala that is running on the ground or just starting to climb a tree.

This koala is actually sleeping in the fork of a tree—another branch is behind its rear end.

15

Eucalyptus leaves do provide a lot of water, though. In fact, they hold almost all the water a koala needs to drink. Every once in a while, a koala might climb down to the ground for a drink. But it doesn't stay on the ground for long! As soon as it can, it climbs back up into the safety of the trees.

Aboriginal (ab-uh-RIJ-uh-nul) people have lived in Australia for thousands of years. The word "koala" is thought to have come from an Aboriginal word meaning "no drink."

Koalas are actually very good swimmers, but they only swim if they have to.

Here you can see a koala that has come down to the ground in search of water.

What Are Baby Koalas Like?

Kangaroos' pouches open at the top, but koalas' pouches open at the bottom. Strong muscles keep the pouch closed so the joey doesn't fall out.

Like other marsupial babies, newborn koalas are very tiny—only about as big as a honeybee!

A newborn koala cannot see and does not even have ears. It has no fur on its body. But it does have strong front legs for crawling. Right after it is born the baby koala, called a *joey*, crawls into its mother's pouch.

This baby koala is only about four or six weeks old. It has started to develop its ears.

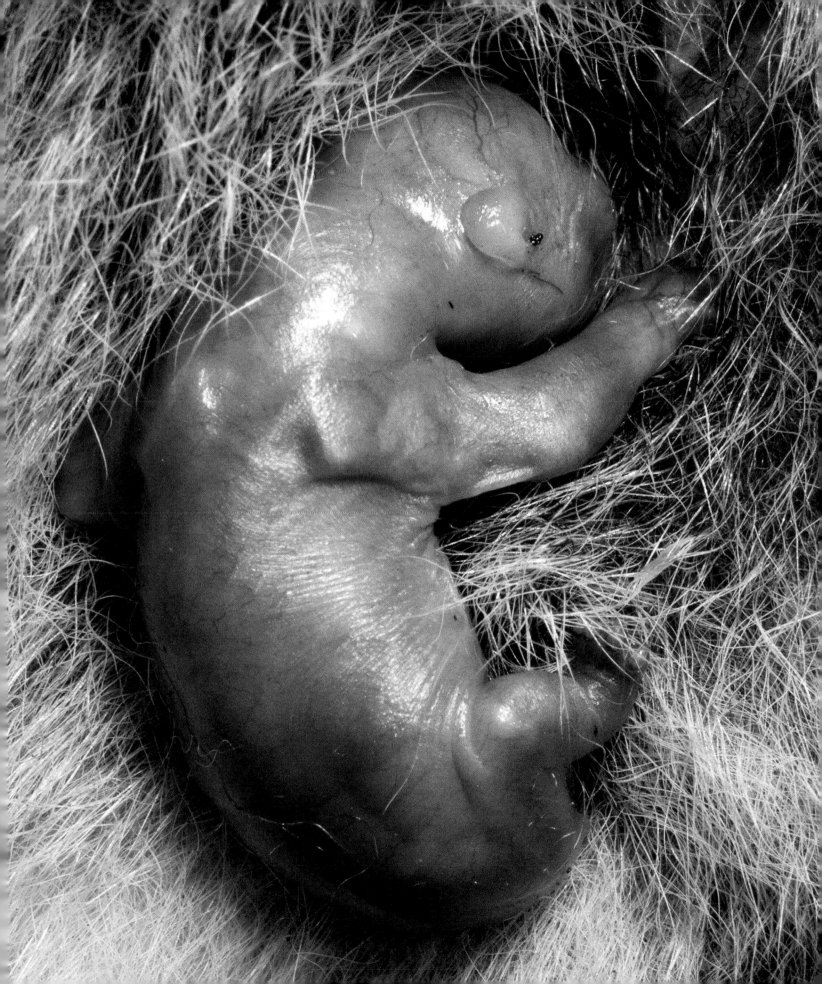

Once the joey is inside the pouch, it hangs onto something that looks like a little finger. It is called a **teat**. Milk from the mother's body comes out of the teat. The joey drinks the milk while it is inside the pouch. Slowly, the joey grows bigger and stronger. After about seven months, it is ready to leave the pouch.

When a joey is about seven months old, its mother starts to produce a mushy paste called *pap*. Pap is made of leaves the mother ate. By eating pap along with its mother's milk, the young joey slowly gets used to eating leaves.

This mother koala is sound asleep. Her joey is asleep in the pouch (its arm is stretched out).

21

After it leaves the pouch, a young koala stays close to its mother. It rides on its mother's head or back wherever she goes. Unlike kangaroo babies, young koalas rarely go back into their mother's pouches—even if they are sleepy or scared. If a koala joey becomes frightened, it holds on to its mother even more tightly.

When it is about a year old, the young koala leaves its mother and finds a new place to live.

You can see how tightly this little joey is clinging to its mother's neck.

After leaving its mother, a joey might stay nearby for another year.

23

Do Koalas Have Any Enemies?

If they can avoid danger and diseases, wild koalas can live to be about 12 years old.

Koalas spend almost all of their lives high in the treetops. There they are safe from most enemies. Sometimes, however, koalas are attacked by large owls, wedge-tailed eagles, pythons, or even giant lizards. Wild dogs called **dingoes** also eat koalas if they find them on the ground.

The koalas' worst enemy, however, is people. Many forest areas where koalas once lived have been destroyed to make room for cities, roads, and farmland. With fewer eucalyptus trees, koalas have less food to eat and fewer places to live. Many koalas are also hurt or killed trying to cross roads to reach new trees.

Adult dingoes like this one stand about 20 inches (51 cm) high at the shoulder and weigh 35 pounds (16 kg). That's about the same size as a border collie. Dingoes eat everything from bugs and mice to rabbits and sheep.

Are Koalas in Danger?

About 100,000 wild koalas are left in Australia.

The Endangered Species List is an official list of the world's animals that are in danger of dying out. Koalas have been on this list in the past. Today, instead of being listed as "endangered," koalas are listed as "threatened." This means their numbers have increased.

In the early 1900s, koalas were hunted for their thick fur. Laws were finally passed to protect koalas from hunters. Even so, the number of koalas stayed low because of the loss of their forest homelands. Today, koalas have made a slight comeback, but they still need people to protect the forests in which they live. If the koalas lose more of their forest areas, they might be in danger of becoming rare once again.

This sign near the Australian city of Adelaide tells drivers to watch for koalas at night.

The people of Australia are now trying to protect koalas. They have set aside special areas with plenty of eucalyptus trees where the koalas can live. These special areas are called **preserves**. In preserves, the eucalyptus trees are safe, too. If people continue to take care of Australia's eucalyptus forests, koalas will be munching leaves for a long, long time.

Koalas might look like quiet animals, but they can be noisy at times. One sound, called a *bellow*, sounds like a mix between a rumbling motorcycle engine and a pig snorting! Koalas grunt when they are angry and scream if they feel scared or threatened. Many people think a koala's scream sounds like the cry of a human baby!

This adult is just about to settle down for an afternoon nap. Doesn't he look sleepy?

29

Glossary

dingoes (DING-ohz) Dingoes are wild dogs that live in Australia. Dingoes sometimes eat koalas that climb down to the ground.

Endangered Species List (en-DAYN-jurd SPEE-sheez list) The Endangered Species List is an official list of the world's animals that are in danger of dying out. Koalas have been on the endangered species list in the past.

mammals (MAM-mullz) Mammals are animals that have warm blood and feed their babies mother's milk. Koalas, dogs, cows, and people are all mammals.

marsupial (mar-SOO-pee-yull) A marsupial is an animal that carries its young in a pouch. Koalas, kangaroos, and opossums are all marsupials.

pouch (POWCH) A pouch is a pocket of skin where marsupial babies live. A female koala's pouch is on her stomach.

preserves (pree-ZURVZ) Preserves are special areas set aside to protect things. In Australia, preserves have been set aside to protect koalas and eucalyptus trees.

teat (TEET) A koala mother produces milk from two teats. They are like baby bottles inside the koala's pouch.

To Find Out More

Watch It!
World of the Koala. VHS. Bethesda, MD: Acorn Media, 1998.

Read It!
Burt, Denise. *Koalas.* Minneapolis, MN: Carolrhoda, 1999.

Dennard, Deborah, and James McKinnon (illustrator). *Koala Country: A Story of an Australian Eucalyptus Forest.* Norwalk, CT: Soundprints, 2000.

Kalman, Bobbie, and Heather Levigne. *The Life Cycle of a Koala.* New York: Crabtree, 2002.

Sotzek, Hannelore, and Bobbie Kalman. *A Koala is Not a Bear!* New York: Crabtree, 1997.

On the Web
Visit our home page for lots of links about koalas:
http://www.childsworld.com/links

Note to Parents, Teachers, and Librarians: We routinely check our Web links to make sure they're safe, active sites—so encourage your readers to check them out!

31

Index

32